VICTORIAN

* GOTHIC *

HOUSE STYLES

Trevor Yorke

COUNTRYSIDE BOOKS
NEWBURY BERKSHIRE

First published 2012
© Trevor Yorke 2012

COUNTRYSIDE BOOKS
3 Catherine Road
Newbury, Berkshire

To view our complete range of books,
please visit us at
www.countrysidebooks.co.uk

ISBN 978 1 84674 304 7

Illustrations by the author

Designed by Peter Davies, Nautilus Design
Produced through MRM Associates Ltd., Reading
Typeset by CJWT Solutions, St Helens
Printed by Berforts Information Press, Oxford

CONTENTS

Introduction

Gothic is a very potent term. It conjures up images of ruined abbeys and castles, horror stories set in misty graveyards, and intense music fans donned in long black coats. Gothic is dark, spooky and atmospheric.

However, 150 years ago it was something far more specific: a new and exciting revival of medieval architecture which displaced the foreign Classical styles as the dominant form of building. It could be colourful, moral and powerful, representing a nation's growing stature and confidence in its indigenous history and future direction. Railway stations, churches, town halls, and the new houses of the upper and middle classes could be designed free from the rules of

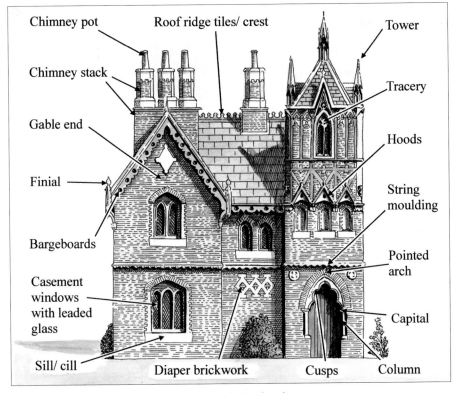

Chimney pot
Roof ridge tiles/ crest
Tower
Chimney stack
Tracery
Gable end
Hoods
Finial
String moulding
Bargeboards
Pointed arch
Casement windows with leaded glass
Capital
Sill/ cill
Diaper brickwork
Cusps
Column

FIG 0.1: *A Victorian Gothic house, with labels of its key parts.*

symmetry, with an honesty in construction and the use of the pointed arch.

Despite the relatively short dominance of this High Victorian Gothic Revival from the late 1840s through to the early 1870s, the ideals of many of its leading lights and the new approach to architecture it initiated were to inspire the next generation of designers and sow the seeds for the later Arts and Crafts movement.

This book sets out to explain the background, introduce the most notable architects and show, using clearly labelled illustrations and my own photographs, the unique features of Gothic Revival houses. The first chapter defines the style, explains how it developed and its effect upon contemporary and later culture. The second chapter describes the finest houses and the work of the leading architects, giving a brief biography of each and examples of their work. The next chapter shows the mass-produced housing which imitated the work of these top designers, the brick semis and terraces which are the familiar face of Gothic Revival in this country. The fourth chapter is packed with photographs of key features and distinctive details which can help identify the style and assist in selecting authentic parts when renovating a house. The final part looks inside at the rooms and describes their original appearance and the style of decoration, furniture and fittings which could be found.

For anyone who simply wants to recognise the style, understand the contribution of key characters and appreciate what makes Gothic houses special, this book makes a colourful and an easy-to-follow introduction to the subject. If the reader is fortunate enough to own such a house, then the illustrations and text will hopefully enlighten them as to its value and aid any planned renovation or redecoration. For those of us who can but look on and admire, I hope the book helps clarify the true essence of the style and why it is such a unique and valuable contribution to a street, a community or even a town, one which is only now being appreciated.

Trevor Yorke
www.trevoryorke.co.uk

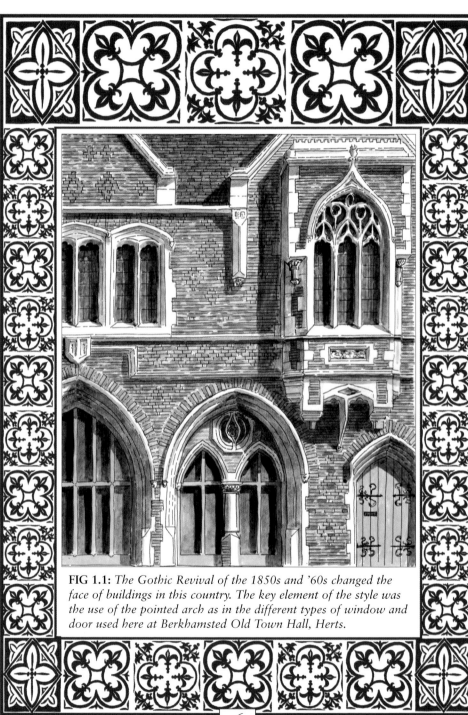

FIG 1.1: *The Gothic Revival of the 1850s and '60s changed the face of buildings in this country. The key element of the style was the use of the pointed arch as in the different types of window and door used here at Berkhamsted Old Town Hall, Herts.*

VICTORIAN
GOTHIC STYLE

Definition and Origins

WHAT IS GOTHIC?

Gothic architecture is character-ised primarily by the use of the pointed arch. Although it is associated with medieval churches, abbeys and cathedrals, and the revival of this style in the 19th century which will be the focus of this book, the pointed arch is a constructional tool not restricted to these periods. As G. E. Street, one of its leading Victorian advocates stated, 'Gothic ... is emphatically the style of the pointed arch and not of this or that nation, or of this or that age'.

However, when his generation of architects studied the buildings of Europe built from the 12th through to the 16th century they were inspired by more than just this more flexible form of arch. The fact that structural elements like buttresses were left exposed on the exterior of medieval churches and, in many cases, embellished with carvings, was an honesty in construction in stark contrast to the Classical style of buildings which was dominant in the early 19th century. The stone and brick used was left in its natural state and, if decorated, was only done so in patterns formed from different coloured types rather than the stucco-covered brick houses which imitated fine masonry in most Victorian cities. The way in which medieval builders arranged the elements of their buildings to suit the requirements of each part, with little concern for the overall appearance, inspired the Revivalists to create asymmetrical façades and free the interior from the restrictive rules of symmetry which had dominated architecture through the 18th century. Inevitably they also used many of the other details which they noted on these medieval buildings, such as battlemented walls, gable ends, pinnacles and towers, not simply copying them but adapting the forms to modern use.

This Gothic Revival from the 1840s through to the 1870s was more than just a passing fashion in building. The nation and its expanding empire were searching for an identity, one that was home-grown rather than inspired by Ancient Greece or Rome. In art and architecture they found it on their doorstep in the soaring cathedrals, colourful paintings and illuminated manuscripts of the Middle Ages. With the rapid changes in society and the effects of the Industrial Revolution, an enfranchised middle class growing in influence sought new moral

FIG 1.2: *The Gothic Revival was most visible in the huge public buildings constructed in towns and city centres during this period of urban expansion, as in these examples from Liverpool, Manchester and Bradford.*

codes and rules and through their rather rose-tinted view of medieval Britain found a time of romantic chivalry, religious adherence and honest craftsmanship. This would inspire not only the ideal Victorian family and the churches they would worship in but also the style of houses they thought fit to live in. Artists and critics began to highlight the faults with the factory system and the poor quality in the design of the goods produced. They recommended the approach of medieval craftsmen who stylised subjects rather than trying to copy them. They began to see an answer to the evils of the Industrial Age in the working practices of guilds and craftsmen from the Middle Ages, although it would not be until later in the century that the Arts and Crafts movement turned the theory into reality.

Before looking at Gothic Revival architecture, the housing produced in imitation of it by builders, the characteristic details on the exterior and how it shaped the inside of the Victorian home, we need to go back and briefly explain where the style originated and why it was brought back to life.

Origins

The Romans are credited with developing the arch (the Greeks only had columns and horizontal lintels to form structures). However, the semi-circular form the Romans used on their Classical buildings was limited in that to make it span a wider space it had to become higher in proportion which was often not convenient. For a bridge or wall this meant that it was usually composed of a series of small arches rather than just a few large ones. Saxon and Norman masons used the same principle in their churches and castles, with very thick walls pierced by small round arches which, although not elegant, have survived through their sheer mass of stonework.

It was only in the late 12th century that a new idea, first seen at Durham Cathedral, developed further in France, and then used by Cistercian monks in the new abbeys they were building in England, was introduced – the pointed arch. This simple device composed of two sections of a larger arch meeting at a point at the top was more flexible in that it could be made wider or thinner like a hinge, without greatly affecting the height of the structure. Its use in buildings over the following three centuries gave master masons greater freedom and, combined with the development of stone ribs, wooden trusses and external buttresses to carry

FIG 1.3: *Saxon and Norman masons used round arches (right) but by the early 13th century the more flexible Gothic pointed arch (left) had been adopted. Note the column on the left is thinner than the pillar in the centre as the use of trusses and buttresses meant wall thickness could be reduced.*

the load from the roof, enabled walls to become thinner and openings larger, thus transforming the interiors of churches and cathedrals into the glorious spaces bathed in colourful light which we admire today.

However, on the Continent during the 15th century, architects were rediscovering the works of Classical antiquity and applying their principles to new buildings. This Renaissance which would affect all forms of art and education changed the approach to building, with the proportions and symmetry of a façade calculated on paper plans rather than scratched on a floor by experienced Gothic masons. In fact, it was in a book written in around 1550 by the Florentine Giorgio Vasari about the work of these new Classical architects that the word 'gothic' was first used. He devised it as a derogatory term, comparing medieval buildings to the Goths, the Northern European tribes who overran the Roman Empire in the 5th and 6th centuries, *'Then arose new architects who after the manner of their barbarous nations erected buildings in that style which we call Gothic'*.

The arrival of the Renaissance in Britain during the first half of the 16th century coincided with the establishment of the Church of England and the Dissolution of the Monasteries. Gothic buildings were being stripped out or demolished and once there was some form of religious and political stability in the reign of Elizabeth I, new houses were erected with symmetrical façades, classical columns and round arches. Wealthy individuals directed their funds towards displays of taste and refinement

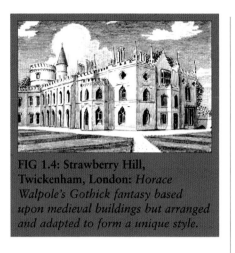

FIG 1.4: Strawberry Hill, Twickenham, London: *Horace Walpole's Gothick fantasy based upon medieval buildings but arranged and adapted to form a unique style.*

through to the late 1770s, transformed a small villa he had purchased in 1747 near the Thames at Twickenham into a Gothic fantasy. Strawberry Hill was the first major domestic building in this revival style, with Walpole's Committee of Taste helping him to design and build the white-rendered structure embellished with battlements, pinnacles and pointed arches adapted from actual medieval structures; the result inspiring a generation of villas, cottages and gatehouses. However, this fanciful style using parts from large buildings and squashing and squeezing them into compact but distorted forms was not a serious attempt to understand the

in country houses, with portraits and collections of books and artwork, rather than looking to the church to guarantee them safe passage through purgatory as their medieval ancestors had done. As a result, few new churches were built after the 1530s and the Gothic style of building had all but died out by the mid 17th century.

Gothick

The revival began in the mid 18th century when the garden designer Batty Langley published *Ancient Architecture Restored and Improved* in 1742 (renamed *Gothic Architecture, improved by Rules and Proportions* in 1747) in which he adapted Gothic forms by applying Classical rules. This resulted in a range of whimsical follies, with only a loose similarity to medieval buildings, appearing in the landscaped gardens of the rich. A more ambitious scheme was devised by Horace Walpole, the fourth son of Prime Minister Sir Robert Walpole who, from the early 1750s

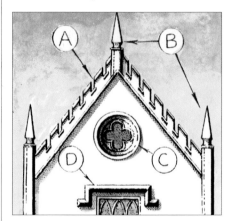

FIG 1.5: *Late Georgian and Regency Gothick houses were distinguished by being covered in stucco (an external render) which was originally painted in beiges and greys to imitate fashionable stone but today are usually white. Other common features were battlements (A), pinnacles and finials (B), quatrefoils (C), and hood moulds above openings (D). Windows often had pointed arches or 'Y'-shaped glazing bars.*

mechanics or motivation behind the originals on which they were based, hence this first phase which reached a peak in the Regency period is known as Gothick.

The Gothic Revival

Attitudes towards medieval architecture began to change from the early 19th century. War with Napoleon had slowed the flow of young aristocrats taking Grand Tours of the classical wonders of Europe while a growing appreciation of the sublime and picturesque inspired many to look at our own historic buildings. Some of the most patriotic created new castles and abbeys in the medieval style and, a little later, Tudor- and Elizabethan-style mansions. At the end of hostilities, artefacts from the Middle Ages flooded the market and collectors began studying manuscripts, illustrations and carvings in more detail, none more so than Augustus Welby Northmore Pugin, the son of a French draughtsman, who began to unravel the principles behind Gothic buildings and set in place practical rules and moral codes which would guide the next generation of architects and artists. His incredible output in such a short life (he died aged 40 in 1852) included designs for the clock tower housing Big Ben in London and the interiors of the Houses of Parliament, churches, country houses, and volumes of drawings and books. These included *Contrasts* (1836) in which he compared contemporary buildings with their medieval equivalents in such a way as to promote his belief that the latter were morally and socially superior.

Pugin was working in a period when the Church of England finally woke up to the changes taking place in society and the rapid expansion of urban areas which had left a large proportion of the population beyond its reach. At the same time the Catholic Emancipation Act of 1829 meant that Catholics too could now worship in public, hence there began a massive church building programme which would last through most of the 19th century (Pugin himself converted to Catholicism in 1834). These buildings, however, would not be the cavernous, box-like chapels with shallow roofs, round-arched windows and symmetrical fronts which had been the standard form for the past century or two. Now, after the Oxford Movement had encouraged the introduction of many medieval practices into the Anglican church, Pugin and the Cambridge Campden Society (later renamed the Ecclesiological Society) promoted Gothic as the most appropriate style for these new churches, more precisely that of the 14th century. They were asymmetrical with towers and spires, ornaments restricted to structural elements, and the division between the nave and chancel now clearly displayed on the exterior, with the walls at first in stone but, by the 1850s, in red brick as it became more acceptable (especially after the repeal of the brick tax in 1850 made it cheaper).

Alongside these were erected new vicarages which reflected the style of the church, with a steep-pitched roof, prominent gables and chimneys, and pointed-arched windows or doors. These buildings looked more like a compact, asymmetrical country house,

FIG 1.6: John Ruskin (1819–1900): *This most inspirational of art critics conveyed his highly moralistic Christian beliefs, love of nature and admiration of medieval Gothic buildings and the craftsmen who built them through a series of influential books, the most notable being* The Stones of Venice *(1853). He promoted Gothic for both its scientific and sacred values, recommended that nature should form the basis of ornamentation, and suggested the use of stepped gables, bargeboards and polychromatic brickwork which he had studied while touring Europe.*

1840s and '50s, the Ecclesiologists were rather elitist and cut off from the main flow of architecture and, although some designed large houses, commercial structures and schools, Classical-based styles still dominated secular buildings. The two different trains of thought erupted into the so-called 'battle of the styles' when a competition was run in 1857 to find an architect for the new foreign office at Whitehall. A selection of Classical and Gothic designs was submitted; the eventual choice being George Gilbert Scott although his plans in the latter style were changed to Italianate under the influence of the Prime Minister, later Lord Palmerston. In the wake of this, Gothic became more prominent with new town halls, offices, factories, universities and country houses built free from the restraints of symmetry and regular spaced windows, with practical red-brick and stone structures featuring spires, steep pitched roofs, pointed arches, and carved medieval motifs rising in most industrial city centres.

These, however, were not in the strict English medieval style laid down by Pugin. By now the influence of the art critic John Ruskin and some of the leading Gothic architects who had all travelled around Europe meant that the style of the 1860s was more flexible, varied and muscular. Colour was introduced with the use of polychromatic brickwork (arches and bands made up of reds, creams and blacks), and more diverse sources of architectural inspiration from places like Venice, Germany and France appeared. It became acceptable to mix elements from different styles on the same

with a tall window breaking through the storeys reflecting that of a medieval hall. At a time when most houses were Classical, Italianate or Tudor in inspiration, these ecclesiastical homes were something of a revelation.

Despite the dominance of the Gothic Revival in church building during the

new Law Courts in London all the entries were based on the Gothic style.

Domestic Revival

This period of so-called High Victorian Gothic, however, was remarkably short-lived. All those multicoloured arches, polished marble columns, lead-covered spires, complicated brickwork and stone carving were expensive and needed specialist craftsmen at a time when most builders had been brought up constructing Classical structures. Gothic had also been attacked in its early days for copyism. The churches of the 1840s and '50s stuck so closely to their 14th-century models that it is still hard for the untrained eye to tell at a glance, the difference between them and their medieval counterparts. It only became common on housing when it lightened up a bit but still not everyone wanted their home to be so ecclesiastical.

FIG 1.7: *Victorian Gothic Revival buildings used features from medieval churches, castles and houses but arranged them in a balanced asymmetrical design. High-quality brickwork, often with colourful patterns formed within the walls as in this house from Ludlow, Salop, is one area where they clearly differ from the originals.*

The next generation of architects who had worked in the practices of some of the most notable Gothic architects began by the late 1860s to look elsewhere for inspiration. Instead of studying medieval churches, they sketched old timber-framed, stone and brick farmhouses, manor houses and large urban buildings from the late 16th and 17th centuries, and adapted their forms and decorative details to create new simplified styles. Sir Richard Norman Shaw and Philip Webb created a number of houses inspired by these sources which merged with the landscape rather than dominating it, their clever designs appearing as if they had developed over centuries while their plan reflected the demands of a modern family. Shaw's Old English style, with

building and, on the largest structures, red-brick skins were wrapped around an iron frame – not the honesty in building which Pugin had advocated. The wealthy middle classes wanted to buy into this new, morally superior style and growing numbers of professional architects were ready to realise their dreams. Further down the scale, local builders erected short rows of terraces with Gothic forms and details applied to their standard plans. Such was the success of this style that in 1867 when a competition was run for designs for the timber-framed gables, low-slung roofs and prominent chimney stacks, was highly influential but did not fit in so well with urban housing. Therefore, the Queen Anne-style was developed using Dutch gables, dormer windows, red-brick and white-painted woodwork (most windows at the time were painted in dark colours or grained to look like wood). These new styles were more homely, adaptable and appealing to the masses, making them popular on suburban houses and terraces. The Gothic style remained dominant for church building although the forms were simplified and structures only bore a loose resemblance to their medieval counterparts.

The Victorian Gothic style is highly distinctive and even today still creates a reaction, positive and negative. Although houses built in its purest form were less popular than the later Queen Anne and Arts and Crafts style of housing, these only developed because of the ground-breaking changes inspired by the likes of Pugin and Ruskin. For nearly 200 years, most terraces and modest houses had been symmetrical, with roofs hidden behind parapets and façades restricted by orders and rules of proportion. Now this Classical dominance had been broken by more flexible asymmetrical plans with gables, roofs and chimneys all on prominent display. Thanks to the work of Victorian Gothic architects, the ideas of honesty in construction, the revival of domestic styles and the fact that the demands of the interior could shape the form of the exterior would inspire later Arts and Crafts and even Modern architects.

FIG 1.9: *A row of Queen Anne-style houses from Bedford Park, West London, a speculative housing development begun in the 1870s aimed specifically at artisans, with the buildings designed by leading architects. This style was distinguished by Dutch gables (top) white-painted woodwork, sash windows, red bricks and terracotta decoration.*

FIG 1.8: *Architects in the 1870s and '80s were inspired by manor and farm houses from the 17th century as in this Olde English-style house from Leek, Staffs, designed by Richard Norman Shaw, with timber-framing above a stone ground floor.*

VICTORIAN GOTHIC HOUSES

Large Houses and their Architects

THE STYLE

The Plan

It is on country houses, vicarages and large urban villas that the Gothic Revival style of the 1850s and '60s was best expressed. These homes were now designed primarily by professional architects rather than builders as many had previously been and, with a more spacious site, they could create asymmetrical structures with a different aspect on each face and a plan determined by the owner's expected use of the rooms within. The houses were also increasingly withdrawing from public gaze as people desired greater privacy. Rather than featuring balconies overlooking the street where one could watch passers-by, the Victorian home was set back behind a brick or stone wall, with an iron gate clearly marking the edge of the property.

Most were rectangular in plan but L-shapes were also used, as well as V-shapes in tight urban sites, with carefully arranged blocks set around a courtyard or central atrium on the largest houses. Gothic houses also had their principal rooms on the ground floor, with the bedrooms above. Although this sounds normal today, most large houses in the 18th century had their drawing and dining rooms on the first floor, sometimes along with the main bedroom. With the need to improve conditions for servants throughout the 19th century and a better understanding of ergonomics, the positioning of the kitchen and its associated service rooms became a key part of the design. Basements in which they had formerly been sited were superseded by carefully arranged service wings or courtyards, while on more modest houses this move

FIG 2.1: Sleaford, Lincs: *An extension to a 15th-century vicarage made in the Gothic style in 1861, with distinctive red-brick asymmetrical façade, gable ends with bargeboards and pointed-arch doorway.*

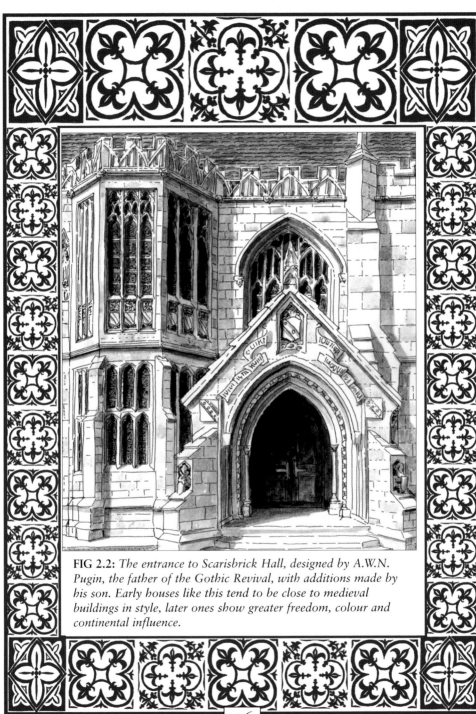

FIG 2.2: *The entrance to Scarisbrick Hall, designed by A.W.N. Pugin, the father of the Gothic Revival, with additions made by his son. Early houses like this tend to be close to medieval buildings in style, later ones show greater freedom, colour and continental influence.*

FIG 2.3: Tyntesfield, Somerset: (National Trust): *This extravaganza of Gothic Revival was built for William Gibbs from 1863 by architect John Norton, with further additions made by Henry Woodyer and Arthur William Blomfield.*

was more generally adopted from the 1870s, with a rear extension the most common place to site the service rooms.

The Structure

Although some architects would state that there was a horizontal element to the façades of their houses, to the untrained eye the emphasis appears to be on the vertical. The pointed arch, spires, tall chimneys and steep-pitched roof direct the eye skywards and the use of towers and tall narrow blocks or wings only increases the effect. The variation in height made for a lively silhouette from whichever angle the building was viewed. This, however, was not just for visual effect. Towers were

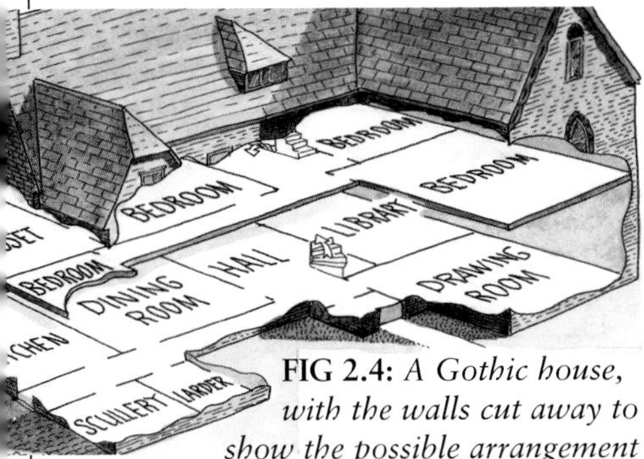

FIG 2.4: *A Gothic house, with the walls cut away to show the possible arrangement of rooms within. Note the large hall and the kitchen within the main house.*

often used in this period to house a storage tank so that it could supply water under pressure to taps below. Some contained staircases and others featured a clock so the family and servants were all working to the same time. Steep-pitched roofs, it was argued, were correct for northern European climates but they also provided more height so servants' quarters could be fitted within, lit by dormer windows with pointed caps. Tall chimney stacks and the fireplace below were often set on the outside of the wall not just to look imposing but to help reduce the fire risk (as they did not pass through the timber roof structure), to buttress the wall, create more space inside and to get a good draw.

The Gothic Revival also resulted in changes to the main façade which rather than being a square or rectangle with a parapet hiding the roof, now had a triangular gable end or two facing the front. The steep roof above was at first covered in plain slate, with a decorative cresting, or featured just a weathervane but very soon the newly-exposed and prominent pitched surfaces were covered in clay tiles formed into bands of different shapes, with elaborate terracotta ridge tiles and decorative

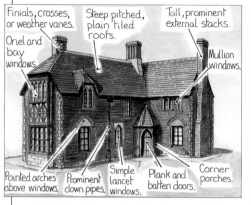

Finials, crosses, or weather vanes.

Oriel and bay windows.

Steep pitched, plain tiled roofs.

Tall, prominent external stacks.

Mullion windows.

Pointed arches above windows.

Prominent down pipes.

Simple lancet windows.

Plank and batten doors.

Corner porches.

FIG 2.5: *A large Gothic vicarage dating from the 1850s, with labels of its key details.*

finials above the ends. Bargeboards edging the top of the gable were also distinctive of this period, carved into decorative patterns, elaborate in this

Gothic period and becoming simpler by the late 19th century.

Windows and doors could be set below a pointed arch. Sometimes they would be manufactured to match the lancet-shaped opening; other times the arch would be formed above or on top of a rectangular feature. Porches became popular, ranging from elaborate medieval church entrances to simpler timber pointed structures, often set at the opposite end of the façade from a gable, or within the corner of an 'L'-shaped plan house.

Materials

Another dramatic change in housing brought about by the Gothic Revival was the return of brick as a facing material. In Tudor and Stuart times it had been a luxury product openly displayed but by the 18th century fine

FIG 2.6: Oxford: *A detached Gothic-style house, with a steep roofed porch designed to complement the gable end above the other end of the façade.*

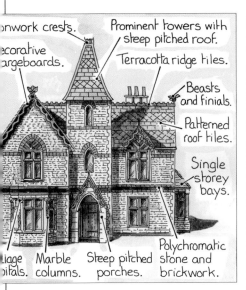

onwork crests.

ecorative
argeboards.

Prominent towers with
steep pitched roof.

Terracotta ridge tiles.

Beasts
and finials.

Patterned
roof tiles.

Single
storey
bays.

Polychromatic
stone and
brickwork.

liage   Marble   Steep pitched
pitals.   columns.   porches.

FIG 2.7: *A façade of a large detached Gothic house dating from the 1860s to '70s, with labels highlighting its key features.*

masonry was more desirable. For those who could not afford it or lived too far from good sources of stone, cheap bricks were used and then covered by a render which was scoured with thin lines and painted to imitate masonry. Although it gave the owner a fashionable exterior, this stucco finish as it was termed covered up all manner of bad practices, especially after a brick tax was introduced in 1784. It was this deceit which so enraged the Gothic Revivalists and although initially they were not too keen on plain brick façades, the promotion of its decorative possibilities by Ruskin and the abolition of the brick tax in 1850 suddenly made it fashionable once again.

In keeping with their belief that pattern should be two-dimensional, different coloured bricks were used to create patterns. At first they were just imitations of 15th- and 16th-century diaper patterns (diamond shapes formed from dark, over-burnt brick ends) but by the late 1850s more colourful polychromatic designs using creams, beiges and black bricks in archways and bands around the house were introduced, becoming distinctive of the following decade. Stone remained popular and it too could be mixed with a different coloured type above openings or used in combination with brick or timber-framing. Ironwork was also used, at first tentatively by Pugin and his contemporaries, but by the 1860s it formed the structure of many of the largest buildings and was widely used for cast-iron decorative details on the exterior, especially along the crest of the roof. Although we think of Gothic buildings as rather dark and foreboding, this is often because a century and a half of grime and soot has covered their original appearance; when cleaned they can be rather like a butterfly emerging from a chrysalis, strikingly bright and colourful.

THE ARCHITECTS

As in this mid Victorian period there was a great demand for new churches, schools, colleges and government buildings, many of the leading Gothic Revival architects of the day, listed on the following pages, produced few domestic properties. However, with the growth of magazines, books and specialist publications, their drawings, plans and thoughts on architecture spread to a wide audience and influenced the design of houses in this style.

William Burges (1827–1881)

Burges was a little less serious than many of his contemporaries who often described him as childlike. A short, stout fellow, he was well aware of his less than enticing appearance, remaining a bachelor all his life. He was clearly a popular, socialite club man, had an opium habit which may have had some effect on his work and had a sense of humour which is reflected in his decorative details. Such was his influence that he was visited on his death bed by Oscar Wilde and James Whistler, and was described by his leading patron's wife as 'Dear Burges, ugly Burges, who designed such lovely things...'

He was the son of a wealthy engineer so, with a guaranteed income, was able to travel across Europe drawing and making notes on architecture and design. He developed his own style, largely based around 13th-century French Gothic, with a wider palette of influence applied to his colourful, imaginative and richly decorated interiors. His period of influence was relatively short. In 1863 he received his first major commission for the new cathedral in Cork, Ireland, but then worked on a wide range of country houses and churches up until his death at the age of 53. The majority of his time, however, was taken up with work for the 3rd Marquis of Bute who, being regarded as the richest man in the country at the time, had not only the wealth to lavish upon Burges's expensive style but also a like mind and similar interest to complement Burges's artistic genius. From 1868 until his death when the work was still incomplete he set about rebuilding Cardiff Castle for Bute. He turned it into the Gothic fantasy it is

FIG 2.8: Cardiff Castle: *The country home of the 3rd Marquis of Bute which was extended by Burges from 1868 to create the huge Gothic structure we see today. In addition to this colossal project, he also renovated nearby Castell Coch for the Marquis, a more fanciful rather than accurate reconstruction of the original 13th-century fortification (see Fig 5.2).*

FIG 2.9: Tower House, Melbury Road, London: *Burges bought a plot of land in the then bohemian Holland Park in 1875 and set about building his own house. It was inspired by 13th-century French Gothic, with the prominent tower after which it is named, similar to those at Castell Coch. The design of the structure and the equally inspirational interiors took up much of Burges's later years and furniture was still being completed when he died in 1881.*

today and at the same time designed the stunning Castell Coch, a smaller fortress further north on the Marquis's estate,

and Park House for Lord Bute's engineer, John McConnochie.

As much as Burges admired Pugin, he had also met with Eugène Viollet-le-Duc, the leading French Gothic architect who believed that function was the starting point of design and was happy to use modern materials in his highly decorative buildings in a style which greatly influenced him. Burges also produced highly decorative pieces of metalwork (including a brooch recently discovered on *Antiques Roadshow* and which sold for £31,000), did much to develop stained-glass window design and lectured on 'Art applied to Industry' a theme which would still be troubling Arts and Crafts designers at the end of the century.

William Butterfield (1814–1900)

Brought up a strict Non Conformist, it is a bit surprising that this leading architect of the Gothic Revival should have dedicated his life to building Anglican churches. He was the most private of men, remaining a bachelor all his life and not even turning up to receive his Gold Medal from the R.I.B.A. in 1884 as he thought it would be 'inconsistent with the habits of his whole life to appear in person publicly'. His buildings ranged from St Paul's Cathedral in Melbourne, Australia, to the Cathedral of the Isles, Great Cumbrae, Scotland, the smallest cathedral in Britain, and also included work on colleges, most notably at Keble in Oxford. Although he produced little domestic work, his Gothic style and use of polychromatic brickwork was highly influential.

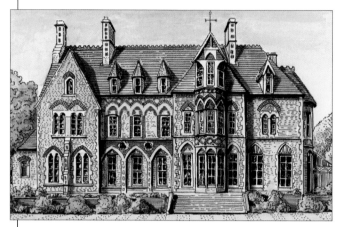

FIG 2.10: Milton Ernest Hall, Beds: *This was the only country house designed by Butterfield (from 1854–58) for the Stacey family to whom he was related by marriage.*

Edward William Godwin (1835–1886)

A largely self-taught architect, he established his own practice in 1854 and as that slowly progressed, he spent much of his time studying Ruskin's *The Stones of Venice* and meeting with William Burges. His early buildings reflect this, with his striking Gothic town halls and work on a number of houses, before he began a relationship with the actress Helen Terry during which he also designed costumes and stage sets. In the late 1860s, Godwin began to integrate Japanese styles into his work; ebonised and geometric pieces of furniture which were a revelation and helped establish the Aesthetic Movement of the 1870s which would flower into the Arts and Crafts in the following decades. He later designed a house for James Whistler, worked for Oscar Wilde and also produced designs for the new Bedford Park estate which would become a showcase for Queen Anne and early Arts and Crafts housing.

William Eden Nesfield (1835–1888)

The son of a notable landscape garden designer, he was articled to the office of

FIG 2.11: Coombe Abbey, near Coventry, Warwicks: *The east wing of this large house was an addition made by Nesfield in the 1860s.*

his uncle, Anthony Salvin, and gained many of his early commissions for work on country houses and lodges from contacts of his father. These buildings incorporated elements reflecting his travels across Europe with the Gothic style of the 1860s. Along with his close friend Richard Norman Shaw, (see *Arts and Crafts House Styles*, published 2011), he then developed a new, more homelier style, based on buildings from south-east England and which developed into the Queen Anne and Old English styles which were widely popular in the following decades.

John Loughborough Pearson (1817–1897)

One of the leading Gothic architects whose work was mainly concentrated upon churches and cathedrals for which he was renowned for his sympathetic handling, elegant verticals and restrained structures. His greatest piece of work was Truro Cathedral, although his designs could be found as far away as Brisbane, Australia, and also included some domestic work as at Quarwood, Gloucestershire.

Augustus Welby Northmore Pugin (1812–1852)

An incredibly dynamic and influential architect and designer who played a key part in promoting Medieval Gothic building and applying it to contemporary structures and interiors. He learnt much about churches from his father, a French immigrant who was an expert on Gothic and worked as a draughtsman for the leading Regency architect, John Nash. Pugin developed a notable collection of medieval artefacts and manuscripts which were a rich source for his designs. As a critic of the Anglicans and then a convert to the newly enfranchised Catholic Church in 1834, his commissions were generally limited to churches of that faith and their associated buildings.

His most notable work was from 1835 when he became an assistant to

FIG 2.12: Quarwood, near Stow on the Wold, Glos: *Designed by Pearson and built from 1856–59 for the Reverend Robert William Hippisley, it combined continental and domestic Gothic themes, with a carefully balanced arrangement. Pearson was not afraid to use plain surfaces as in this example, unlike most Victorians who revelled in decoration. (This private house has since been largely altered and this view is of its original appearance).*

Charles Barry in the rebuilding of the Houses of Parliament. He was chosen for his knowledge of Gothic architecture (even though he was only in his early twenties) and was responsible for most of the interior designs, with the spectacular Chamber of the House of Lords completed in 1847 being his most influential masterpiece. It was also of note that he assembled around him craftsmen and manufacturers who themselves would rediscover and develop ways of producing authentic medieval carvings, carpentry and decorative materials like tiles and fabrics. This was against the contemporary flow of mass production and would be influential to later generations of architects.

His greatest contribution to the spread of Gothic architecture came in his writings, arguing that the style was both morally and aesthetically superior to the dominant Classical style, citing the buildings of the 14th century as the most appropriate to form the basis for new structures. Although the limited pallet this provided for architects soon forced them to look elsewhere for inspiration, his key principles on design were longer lasting, inspiring later generations. These included his belief that any features on a building should be serving a purpose, so columns, buttresses or brackets should actually be supporting something and not be hidden from view and that decoration should be limited to the enrichment of these parts and not consist of pilasters (half columns stuck to a façade) or raised mouldings which served no purpose. He also revolutionised design in pointing out the way that medieval masons did not copy foliage directly but simplified and stylised it

FIG 2.13: St Giles church, Cheadle, Staffs: *One of Pugin's finest pieces in that he had a generous benefactor and a budget which enabled him to complete the project much as he had planned. John Talbot, the Earl of Shrewsbury, was a passionate promoter of the Catholic Church and he first employed Pugin in 1837 to work on his principal residence Alton Towers (the house still at the centre of the modern-day theme park) and buildings in the adjoining village. In 1841 work began on his church in nearby Cheadle. It took five years to complete and was inspired by buildings Pugin had visited in Norfolk, Antwerp and Paris. The materials mainly came from local quarries and trees on the Earl's estate.*

FIG 2.14: The Grange, Ramsgate, Kent: *The house which Pugin built for himself and his family, completed just a couple of years before his death. It epitomised his architectural doctrine with honesty in its construction and the function of the rooms reflected in the arrangement of windows (note the three small openings above each other on the tower marking the staircase and the lower bay window illuminating the library where he carried out his designs).*

carefully to fill the vacant space. He also stated that surfaces should consist of two-dimensional patterns and not the contemporary fashion for false relief with shading in wallpapers and fabrics.

Shortly after completing the Gothic Court at the Great Exhibition of 1851 which was heralded by critics as 'successfully applying Medievalism to the present day', he suffered health problems. The following year after a breakdown he died on 14th September 1852, aged only 40.

George Gilbert Scott (1811–1878)

Sir George Gilbert Scott designed over 800 buildings in this country, of which over three quarters are today protected as of historic value. He built some of the finest buildings of the Victorian Age here and around the Empire, helped restore eighteen of our cathedrals and yet is probably the most uncelebrated and unappreciated of British architects. His reputation suffered almost immediately after his death in 1878 when William Morris and his followers began criticising Gilbert Scott's restoration methods, claiming he had destroyed much of the medieval churches he was meant to be saving by replacing original parts with his version of Gothic. It reflects a debate which continues to this day on whether old buildings should be conserved or restored. However, Scott was working at a time when these ancient buildings were not fully appreciated and his actions in returning them to practical fully functioning edifices certainly saved many which would have otherwise collapsed. (Some he worked on already had had parts of them collapse.)

FIG 2.15: The Albert Memorial, Kensington, London: *Designed by Scott in memory of Prince Albert who died in 1861.*

The son of a clergyman, he was criticised at a young age by one of the architects he studied who said he 'wasted his time sketching medieval buildings'. His first commissions were for workhouses, of which, with his colleague William Bonython Moffatt, he designed over forty in Classical, Elizabethan and Jacobean styles. He became involved with the Ecclesiological Society and was influenced by Pugin (on the frieze of architects on his Albert Memorial he puts himself respectfully behind Pugin) and began his prolific career of designing and restoring churches and cathedrals here and across the globe. In his 1857 publication *Remarks on Secular and Domestic Architecture, Present and Future*, he emphasised his belief in the style of Gothic as something flexible and modern, not simply copying the past.

His was a more relaxed and practical approach than Pugin's and had a huge influence on the work of others in the following decades. Around the same time he was wrangling with Prime Minister Lord Palmerston over the design for the new Foreign Offices. The much debated 'Battle of the Styles' between Gothic and Classical eventually ended in a compromise of Italianate, and the building still stands today. He also found time to design a number of domestic properties, mainly vicarages and parsonages associated with churches he was working on, plus a number of country houses and even workers' cottages.

His two most memorable pieces the Albert Memorial and the Midland Hotel, St Pancras, both in London, have recently been restored to their former glory as today his tremendous output

FIG 2.16: Midland Hotel, St Pancras, London: *Built around an iron frame, with 13th-century French Gothic as a theme. This most striking of Victorian Gothic buildings was designed by Scott combining uniformly spaced windows and decorative details, with an asymmetrical structure to reflect the awkward shaped site.*

FIG 2.17: The University of Wales, Aberystwyth: *This imposing Gothic structure designed by Seddon in the early 1860s was originally intended to be the Castle Hotel but was too large and so became part of the University of Wales.*

and loving skill in handling Gothic buildings is beginning to be appreciated. It is also of note that two of his sons went on to become architects and his grandson Giles designed Liverpool's Anglican Cathedral, the Tate Modern building, Battersea Power Station, and the telephone box!

John Pollard Seddon (1827–1906) and John Pritchard (1817–1886)

These two architects formed a partnership between 1852 and 1863 when they produced a number of Gothic buildings and worked on the restoration of Llandaff Cathedral, Cardiff, and

FIG 2.18:Ettington Park, near Stratford-upon-Avon, Warwicks: *This country house designed by Pritchard for E.P. Shirley was built from 1858–63 and is now a hotel. Its colourful stone work, arches and towers have Italian influence as advocated by Ruskin.*

other churches. From 1858 Pritchard also remodelled Ettington Park, Warwickshire, in a dramatic Gothic style. Meanwhile Seddon produced the equally bold Castle Hotel, Aberystwyth, in the early 1860s, which was so vast in concept that it never opened as originally planned but instead became part of the University College of Wales.

George Edmund Street (1824–1881)

Although educated to follow his father as a solicitor, Street turned his attention to architecture after his father died in 1840 and worked under George Gilbert Scott for a number of years before establishing his own practice in 1849. He was a highly skilled draughtsman and made many studies of medieval buildings and his *Brick and Marble in the Middle Ages: Notes of a Tour in Italy* of 1855 helped make poly-chromatic brickwork, as advocated by Ruskin, popular in the following decade. Most of his output was directed towards church building and restoration although he also designed numerous vicarages and a number of secular buildings. His most notable achievement was winning the competition for the Law Courts in London, a huge undertaking for which it was rumoured he produced around 3,000 drawings and which was blamed for his early death at the age of 57. His final years were spent in the Surrey village of Felday (now named Holmbury St Mary after the church which Street built there). His wife Mariquita had fallen in love with Felday and he built a house for them there called Holmdale, only for Mariquita to pass away two years later. He remarried in 1876 but his new bride fell ill on their honeymoon and died shortly after.

He was a much revered character, becoming President of the Royal Institute of British Architects and is buried in Westminster Abbey close to G.G. Scott and Charles Barry. He is also of note in that the next generation of

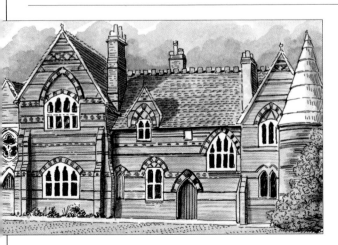

FIG 2.19: Boyne Hill, Maidenhead, Berks: *Part of a complex of church, vicarage, school, clergy house and almshouses designed by Street, with the place of worship consecrated in 1857. It is an early use of polychromatic brickwork.*

FIG 2.20: Hutton in the Forest, Cumbria: *The south-east tower in this picture was an addition by Anthony Salvin who, like many of his generation, was happy to work in a number of styles although most of his domestic work was in the form of medieval fortified buildings as in this example. Note the pointed arches and stylised battlements and how it contrasts with the earlier Classical structure to the right.*

leading architects and designers, including William Morris, Philip Webb, and Richard Norman Shaw, began their careers in his practice.

* * * *

Other notable architects in this period who worked in the Gothic Revival style included Anthony Salvin (1799–1881), whose work on country houses was mostly in the form of castles or Tudor mansions; Samuel Saunders Teulon (1812–1873); and Edward Buckton Lamb (1806–1869) who built churches and country houses in this style. Alfred Waterhouse (1830–1905) was not known for domestic work but produced some of the finest buildings of this High Victorian period, most notable being Manchester Town Hall (see Fig 1.2) and the Natural History Museum, London.

In America, Alexander Jackson Davis was a leading advocate of the Gothic Revival in a series of fine houses and worked for a while with Andrew Jackson Downing who later popularised a form of Picturesque Gothic through his writings and designs. Downing, like Pugin, believed that '... no principle of utility will be sacrificed to beauty, only elevated and ennobled by it', but unfortunately he also died young when he was killed at the age of 36, along with 80 others in a boat fire on the Hudson River.

VICTORIAN GOTHIC HOUSING

Semis, Terraces and Estate Houses

Early and Mid Victorian housing

Away from the architect-designed country houses and urban villas, the bulk of housing was erected by small-scale builders. They would put up a row of perhaps three or four houses and then

FIG 3.1: *The point where one phase of building or a different builder took over can be spotted in terraces as in this example marked by the two yellow arrows. The windows here have 'Y'-shaped glazing bars which are distinctive of Gothick houses from the early 19th century.*

usually wait to be paid for their work, receive rent or sell the buildings themselves before moving on to the next project. Although a terrace can appear to be all of one date, on closer inspection you can often see in the brickwork or decoration where one batch finished and the next one began. There were a few larger companies and some housing schemes in which a landlord would employ an architect to oversee a model village or large commercial project, but in general it was these small companies and individual builders who were responsible for developing the rapidly expanding middle-class Victorian suburbs.

With money so tight they could not afford to take risks, yet at the same time, they were building for a class who, through magazines, books and museums, were becoming more aware of architectural fashions and were demanding something other than just a brick box. The basic plan of the terraced house remained the same, with a front and rear room, bedrooms above (no bathroom at this date) and a narrow hall to the side to differentiate it from the top end of the working-class stock. However, the façade and the decorative details applied to it could be altered to suit the style which would appeal best to

FIG 3.2: *On the more modest middle-class terraces, the Gothic style was often subtly introduced, with pointed arches and patterns formed in the brickwork as in these examples.*

FIG 3.3: *The area just north of Oxford City centre was developed from the mid 19th century and is one of the best places to see Gothic style houses dating mainly from the 1860s and '70s.*

potential tenants (the vast majority of people rented their homes until the early 20th century). In the 1830s and '40s the Classical styles still dominated so plain brick or rendered fronts, with regularly spaced sash windows and a parapet above to hide the roof, was the most popular form, with a few reflecting the fashion for Elizabethan or Picturesque Cottage styles. Even in the 1850s when the Gothic Revival churches were being erected in every town, most houses were still being built with Classical or a new Italianate style popularised by Queen Victoria's Osborne House on the Isle of Wight, with sets of two or three round-arched windows, low-pitched slate roofs and deeply overhanging eaves.

FIG 3.4: *A row of houses from Huddersfield built in the three dominant styles of the early and mid Victorian period, Classical on the left, Gothic in the middle and Italianate on the right.*

FIG 3.5: *Builders could buy in stone mouldings from catalogues and local merchants and apply them to houses, as around the door, window and gable in this example. Note also how this building at Stoke on Trent fits into a narrow-angled site, a common arrangement in Victorian towns for which the Gothic style was ideally suited.*

Gothic terraces and semis

As Gothic secular buildings and country houses began to appear during the 1850s and the influence of Ruskin and leading architects spread to a wider audience, so the middle classes began to take notice of this new style. It was one which reflected their new ideals that life should be centred around the family and Christianity. There were other changes which also made this new style accessible to the masses. The repeal of the tax on bricks in 1850 made them cheaper and it became acceptable to put them on show rather than have them hidden behind render, especially in the 1860s when polychromatic patterns were all the rage. Stone also became widely available and dropped in price as the railways developed and quarrying methods improved, with machine-cut stone mouldings, columns and decorative carvings being bought by builders through local merchants or trade catalogues. An increasing number of pattern books and trade magazines contained plans and illustrations which helped spread the new style and could be understood by tradesmen unfamiliar with the more complex aspects of architecture.

Unlike in the larger architect-designed house where the demands of the interior could shape the exterior, the builder usually would not know whom his tenants would be so he stuck to familiar plans and structures. The façade, however, did change to suit the new style, with gable ends facing out, trimmed with decorative bargeboards, while the now exposed steep-pitched roof above could feature patterned bands and terracotta ridge tiles. With the abolition of the

FIG 3.6: Huddersfield, South Yorks: *A standard form of Victorian semi-detached or terraced house with entrance and hall to one side, drawing room at the front and dining room behind it at the rear. Basements were still common in this class of house up until the 1870s and timber or stone porches also often featured. Note that with the limited height the sashes are tucked behind the stone arches in the bay and first-floor windows.*

FIG 3.7: *A drawing of a large London terrace, with labels showing how the builder used details from various styles to make a characteristic mid Victorian eclectic mix.*

thic
bles.

lianate
ves.

othic
ch and
otif.

assical
buldings.

lianate
indows.

uskin
spired
ickwork.

lassical
ediments.

window tax and improvements in the mass production of glass, bay windows which had previously been too expensive for this class of housing were now a common fitting. They were usually only on the bottom storey at this date except on the finest housing, not spreading up both storeys until the late 19th century. This gave the builder the opportunity to fit stone columns with carved foliage capitals to the sides of the windows, a decorative detail which could also be applied to external porches, another popular addition in this period. Decorative brickwork patterns and bands of different coloured bricks were

FIG 3.8: *Although reviving the past, the Gothic style could equally be applied to buildings of the future. This house from Lordship Lane, Dulwich, London, dates from the early 1870s and was one of the earliest examples built in concrete more than 50 years before it became a fashionable material. Despite its historic importance, this house has been derelict for years and has only recently been listed and saved from demolition.*

easy to incorporate and were often used even to lift the façade of more basic terraces. Middle-class housing also began to be stepped back from the road, with small front gardens behind a low wall with mass-produced cast-iron railings and gates now available to help separate the family from the outside world.

There were problems, however, with the Gothic style which limited its appeal and which was deemed by many purists not suitable for terraced housing. The leaded lights set in mullions or custom-made windows used in the finest housing were expensive, so builders wanted to use ordinary rectangular sash windows. There were also problems fitting the pointed arch in these lower height houses. Builders could make an impression of it in the brickwork above openings but often there was not sufficient room. A compromise was to fit a pointed arch over the top sash which slid up behind it, a more complex and potentially trouble-some method. As a result, most housing in this mid Victorian period tends to contain an eclectic mix of styles, with the Gothic Revival freeing the façade from obsessive symmetry, bringing the gable to the fore and making colourful displays of brickwork fashionable but at the same time being found alongside Italianate windows or Classical parapets. It would not be until the late 1870s when the Old English and Queen Anne style became fashionable that builders found a more adaptable approach which could be easily and economically applied to the whole façade.

Estate housing

This was a time when 'self help' was the

order of the day; people were regarded as responsible for their own position in society even if a large proportion were born into a poverty trap. There were no councils to provide housing and governments turned their back on the problem. The standard of housing for the urban masses was generally poor and huge swathes of towns and cities were slums and no-go areas for the better off, and, surprisingly, things were often worst in the country. The first notable improvements in housing for the working classes came when a few benevolent factory owners, religious families and charitable groups began to erect more spacious, clean homes which could range from a short terrace to small housing estates or model villages. These would still be regarded as basic by modern standards and often tied the tenants to a business, church adherence and higher rents. Those developing the larger estates would usually bring in an architect to oversee the scheme and a suitable style would be chosen for the housing. During the 1850s and '60s many of these small rows of workers' cottages or model

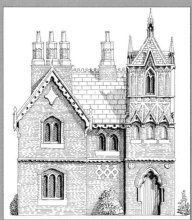

FIG 3.9: Two examples of estate building: Holly Village, Highgate, London (left) and Akroydon, Halifax (right). *Although both are built in the Gothic style, the latter was intended to house mill workers and the former was built for wealthy tenants as a small country retreat. Akroydon was planned as an extensive estate of 350 houses, designed by George Gilbert Scott from 1859 and, unusually, the houses were for sale rather than rent. In the end, only 92 were built and the cost was such that very few mill workers could afford to buy them. Holly Village was the brainchild of Baroness Burdett-Coutts (1814–1906), a wealthy but passionate philanthropist who is alleged to have been described by Edward VII as 'After my Mother (Queen Victoria), the most remarkable woman in the country'. This small community was sold to its tenants in 1921 and remains a unique private enclave surrounded by suburban housing to this day.*

villages were built in a Gothic style, ranging from plain façades broken by a few pointed arches to cottage-style buildings with a wealth of decorative bargeboards and vernacular materials.

In the countryside a large number of estate villages had been partially or fully rebuilt since the 18th century, often when a new landscape park was being laid out which engulfed the old settlement. Although some were built with fanciful Classical details, many were inspired by more traditional English models, with exaggerated long thatched roofs and pretty little windows in a style known as Cottage Orne. In 1833 J. C. Loudon, a notable botanist and landscape designer, published the *Encyclopaedia of Cottage, Farm and Villa Architecture*, an influential collection of designs for estate housing designed to 'improve the standard of dwellings for the great mass of society'. It became an important reference for architects and builders over the coming decades and played a part in the development of the Tudor and Gothic styles of cottage, with decorative bargeboards, hanging tiles or timber-framed upper storeys, mullion or casement windows and prominent chimney stacks. If the landlord who financed it was more generous, then the houses could become a riot of pointed arches, Gothic motifs and carved stonework. Others were more economical, with most of the budget going on external appearance rather than the facilities inside.

FIG 3.10: *The Gothic, Tudor and Cottage Orne styles were popular for lodges and gatehouses, especially in the first half of the 19th century. This example from Leek, Staffs, has Gothic-style roof tiles, bargeboards, and exposed red brick, with Tudor-style windows and chimneys. Many of these compact houses have survived long after the mansion or institution they stood at the entrance of has gone and can often be found engulfed by later housing estates.*

FIG 3.11: *Many country house owners relocated and rebuilt estate villages in order to make more attractive approaches to their homes and to provide better housing for selected staff. At Ilam, Staffs, a number of cottages like these were designed by George Gilbert Scott and still make a romantic setting to the now ruined hall.*

VICTORIAN GOTHIC DETAILS

Doors, Windows and Decoration

The Victorians loved decorative surfaces. Those who had the money to spend wanted a house which would project their position in society and were happy for builders to pack the façade with an eclectic mix of busy patterns, intricate carvings and intense colours. From the 1850s through into the 1870s Gothic windows, doors, columns, bargeboards and decorative details were custom-made for some of the finest houses or mass produced and applied to standard urban villas and terraces.

Most carvings were made from stone or brick, some terracotta mouldings were available although this is a material which came to prominence upon the façade of houses in the 1880s and '90s. Although oak was desirable most wood used in doors, windows and bargeboards was softwood, not the cheap modern types from the outer parts of fast growing trees but the heartwood from mature trees creating a timber which has lasted over a century and with repair and painting will last many more. It is also worth noting that bright white gloss paints were not available in this period, so most external timber work

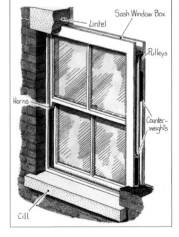

FIG 4.1: Window horns: *There were significant changes to sash windows during the early and mid Victorian period. With the mass production of larger sheets of glass, the price dropped and windows with just four, two and eventually one single pane of glass could be found in each sash. Without the glazing bars to stiffen the frame it became weak and could distort so, to counter this, the junction between the sides of the top sash were extended down to make the joint with the bottom bar stronger. These extensions called horns were usually finished with a simple moulding and can help to identify windows from this period onwards for, when making replicas of earlier styles, carpenters still tended to put them on even when glazing bars were fitted.*

FIG 4.2: *Despite the emphasis by leading architects upon balance, form and function, the most striking part of many Victorian Gothic Revival houses are the decorative details on the exterior.*

was grained or painted a mid or dark brown to imitate hardwood, with a colour like a dark green or black limited to doors and metalwork.

FIG 4.3: Windows with tracery: *In the finest houses a window with carved stone patterns in its upper section called tracery could be found illuminating an important room. These tend to be on large country houses or vicarages but can be found elsewhere and generally copy designs found upon late 13th- and early 14th-century churches. Stained glass was often fitted with heraldic designs although it was not widely used until the late 1800s when mass-produced coloured glass patterns could be found in the doors and windows of middle-class terraces.*

FIG 4.4: Sash windows with pointed-arch frames: *In the finest houses pointed-arched sash windows could be made specifically for a house or an estate. Alternatively, fixed frames with an opening section (a casement) could be fitted although these sometimes turn out to be modern replacements for sashes.*

FIG 4.5: Sash, with rectangular frame behind pointed arch: *Another popular way of introducing the pointed arch was to build it across the top of a rectangular sash window (a deceit which purists would not have approved of). These were widely available and cheaper than casement types so the only complication for the builder was constructing the arch on the outer skin. It was also common for these to be grouped in twos or threes and have a column between them (see Fig 4.17). Another method was to form the shape of an arch in the brickwork above the rectangular opening (see Fig 4.19 for examples).*

FIG 4.6: Dormer windows:
Now that the roof was exposed, any windows set within it to illuminate the attic had to be more decorative. Dormer windows which are vertical frames with a little roof and sides finished off with bargeboards were usually fitted. Some were set fully within the roof (left), others only partially (right).

FIG 4.7: Bay and oriel windows: *With the abolition of the window tax, bays (which rested upon the ground, bottom right) and oriels (which were raised off it, bottom left) became fashionable, even on modest middle-class terraces. At this date bay windows were usually on the ground floor only, with a parapet above, either plain (top centre), decorated (bottom right) or with battlements (top right). If there was space above, a steep pitched roof could be fitted (top left).*

FIG 4.8: Porches: *Porches with steep-pitched roofs are a distinctive feature of Gothic Revival houses. They range from fully enclosed types to timber hoods (left) and their design often complemented a gable above it on the façade. Ones which were recessed within the house became popular on middle-class houses from the 1870s.*

FIG 4.9: *Examples of Gothic Revival porches.*

FIG 4.10 Doors: *A characteristic of Gothic houses was the use of a pointed arch for the doorway. Within this a door formed from vertical planks facing outwards and horizontal battens across the inner face (plank and batten door) were the most common type fitted. Panelled doors, with coloured or etched glass upper sections, became popular from the 1870s. Doors were usually left in their natural colour if made from a hardwood like oak, were stained to look like these if of softwood, or were painted in a strong colour.*

FIG 4.11: Door furniture: *Originally, most Gothic Revival doors would have had black-painted iron strap hinges, (which could become quite elaborate as in this example), and knockers and knobs (handles become popular in the late 19th century). Wrought iron was advocated by Gothic architects although mass-produced cast-iron versions were more generally used. On middle-class villas and semis, a wider range of door styles could be found, often with brass knobs and knockers which were seen as acceptable.*

FIG 4.12: Bargeboards: *One of the most distinctive features of Gothic houses are the decorative wooden strips which cover the eaves of gables. These bargeboards were usually carved in a variety of patterns, often with openings or perforations. Later types from the late 19th and early 20th century tend to be simpler in design with no cut outs. It is also important to note that they were often applied to older buildings, so it is quite common to find these elaborate bargeboards fitted on humble cottages that originally would have had nothing more than plain boards.*

FIG 4.13: Motifs: *Medieval motifs like the four-lobed quatrefoil (top left) were often found within decorative metalwork or stone carving. Terracotta plaques and exterior glazed tiles became popular from the 1870s.*

FIG 4.14: Terracotta ridge tiles: *Bands of decorative roof tiles with a capping of terracotta ridges were popular in the 1860s and '70s. These would usually have a finial in terracotta, stone or metal, or an elaborate carved beast like a dragon mounted on the end of the gable.*

FIG 4.15: Guttering and rainwater traps: *Cast-iron rainwater traps at the top of vertical lengths of guttering were now prominent on the front of houses so it was common for a simple Gothic design to be cast onto them.*

FIG 4.16: Gates: *As the house was set further back from the public road, so walls, hedges and railings were erected to enclose it. Railings were usually set in holes with lead and only had a horizontal bar along the top; most replicas have them top and bottom. Cast-iron gates with Gothic motifs or a pointed arch were also common.*

FIG 4.17: Columns and capitals: *Stone columns (marble in some of the finest examples), with a capital on top carved with foliage patterns, were a popular feature between windows and around doorways. They imitated those which formed the aisles in medieval churches and could be ordered from catalogues or local suppliers and simply fitted by the builder on site. Although some could be quite elaborate, leading Gothic architects advocated simpler, stylised designs.*

47

FIG 4.18: Chimneys: *Chimneys became prominent features on Gothic houses, often with the whole stack protruding from the wall, thus freeing up space inside. Tudor style ones were popular (left) but on most true Gothic houses the individual chimney was relatively simple, with the interest coming from its position and form (right).*

FIG 4.19: Brickwork patterns: *Late medieval and Tudor brick houses used the grey ends of over-burnt bricks to form diaper patterns (diamonds), something which was copied on early Victorian Gothic red-brick houses. Ruskin introduced the idea of making colourful two-dimensional designs in his book* The Stones of Venice, *and polychromatic bands and patterns are distinctive of the 1860s and '70s.*

VICTORIAN GOTHIC INTERIORS

Fixtures and Fittings

As Charles Eastlake pointed out in his influential 1868 book *Hints on Household Taste in Furniture, Upholstery and Other Details*, most householders were stuck with the façade of their urban terrace and could do little to change it so should concentrate their decorative efforts upon the interior. As most people rented and any changes to the narrow front of a house would be expensive and problematic so the interior walls, floors, and fittings were a more suitable canvas to express their taste and ambitions with the latest Gothic style. Eastlake's book, along with others at the time, was fighting a battle against what was seen as poor design. Most of the people creating mass-produced furniture, fittings and decoration had little education in the subject and those buying it even less. Poorly-constructed

FIG 5.1: *Gothic Revival interiors could be colourful and rich as in these examples from Burges's church at Studley Royal, nr Ripon, Yorks (on the Fountains Abbey estate). In these finest interiors, painted ceilings inspired by Christian and Islamic examples and polished coloured marble columns were distinctive features.*

FIG 5.2: *Gothic interiors could range from the spectacular masterpieces of architects like William Burges, as in this example from Castell Coch, to modest drawings rooms in a terrace, which would be crammed with strong colours, busy patterns and an overwhelming number of ornaments.*

goods overwhelmed with decorative motifs or novelty products which hid their true purpose were being crammed into every available nook and cranny of a home, with little control over the whole effect. Although today it is the simplified patterns and beautifully balanced interiors of leading architects and designers which we are familiar with from houses we visit and books we read, it is likely that most Gothic-style interiors at the time were far from refined.

There was, however, some reasoning behind this apparent madness and clutter. Busy patterns and strong colours were picked for downstairs rooms because the atmosphere outside was filthy, coal dust blew in every time the door was opened and mud and muck from unmade roads was brought in with every step across the threshold. Most middle-class houses were also much busier than they are today. There was traffic from the extended family, servants going to and fro with tasks, and a constant stream of guests and tradesmen so surfaces had be durable and hide the dirt. These bold and dark

fabrics, papers and tiles, however badly they were designed, were seen as exciting and exotic to many but had only been made practical with the spread of brighter gas lighting and the introduction of new colour dyes for printing from the late 1850s.

With no culture of interior design, DIY shops or TV makeover programmes, the average middle-class family who had recently risen to this status had neither the information nor inclination to concern itself with good design. They usually left decorating to professionals, with the lady of the house just choosing colours or patterns. The furnishings and fittings emblazoned with motifs or mouldings satisfied their desire to display their relative wealth and love for decoration. The fact that they were positioned upon walls with such rich patterns that the two clashed rather than complemented each other or were grained in imitation of better-quality woods seems to have been of little concern to many.

It was only from the 1870s that the work of designers like Charles Eastlake, Owen Jones and William Morris began

FIG 5.3: Cliffe Castle Museum, Keighley, Yorks: *Stained glass based upon medieval designs was a feature of the finest homes, often casting light over the hall or staircase. Although similar to the originals, you can often identify Victorian work by the style of the figure's hair as with these clearly 19th-century gentlemen. This museum contains an outstanding display of Victorian stained glass.*

FIG 5.4 : *A late Victorian interior, with labels highlighting the key parts.*

to influence a new generation of professionals who started producing simplified products and creating more tasteful interiors for a clientele which, through new magazines and shops, began to appreciate their work. The cluttered and dark mid Victorian interior was still a familiar sight, though, well into the 20th century. In this chapter I outline how each room was likely to have appeared at the time and illustrate the furnishings and fittings which were available. For those who are recreating a Gothic interior, these will perhaps give some background ideas. However, only a few original fabrics, papers and tiles are available now so hints on where to find these and

reproductions of them can be found in the Appendix at the end of the book.

THE ROOMS

Hall

Away from large country houses the hall had become rather a forgotten passageway, somewhere to pass through to get to the staircase which would lead you up to the grand reception rooms above. For some, this changed during the early Victorian period as Gothic Revivalists brought back the idea of a medieval hall, not the cavernous space at the centre of the house but a large sitting room which could be used to welcome guests and be spacious enough for

FIG 5.5: *The hall of a larger urban house, with the extra width enabling margin lights either side of the front door, pieces of furniture for visitors and a compact fireplace to be fitted. Note the geometric patterned tiled floor which is so distinctive of this period.*

festivities. These new square halls could be found in some larger Gothic-style houses and were built with wooden panelling (oak or mahogany in the finest, painted or grained softwoods in the cheaper examples), beamed ceilings, seating, a table, a fireplace and perhaps a large window featuring stained-glass designs in the most luxurious examples. This also reflected the change in the arrangement of the interior at the time as the main reception rooms were moved downstairs and the hall was now

flanked by dining and drawing rooms, with the stairs now only leading up to family bedrooms and hence a less prominent feature.

For most in urban houses, where space was at a premium, the hall remained a narrow passage. In some, though, especially later in the 19th century, they could be wider, with glass panels flanking the front door. The walls and floors had to be durable and disguise the muck that was going to be brought in so dado rails were usually fitted, with wooden panelling, ceramic tiles or an embossed paper below and patterned encaustic or geometric tiles underfoot. Although plain walls were often advocated by designers, patterned papers were usually fitted on the upper wall, strong-coloured if there were glass panels in the door or to the side, lighter stone, greys, creams and greens if there was only a fanlight. The main load-bearing wall spanning the house was carried across the hall usually by an arch and this could often feature Gothic foliage-style capitals at each end. The owner would then try and fit in as many furnishings as possible like an umbrella and coat-stand, a compact fireplace, a tall case (grandfather) clock, and a small table and chair so that guests and tradesmen could sit and wait to be called in to see the owner or leave their calling card. It was also common for a thin rug to be laid down covering and protecting the patterned flooring, only being removed when important guests were expected. In wider examples, the owner may have tried to imitate a medieval hall, with heraldic symbols, armour and stuffed animal heads.

FIG 5.6: *With the constant battering that the walls took from the family and guests, as well as the dirt and grime which was dragged in from unmade streets, they had to be finished with a material which was durable and could hide marks. Embossed papers, ceramic wall tiles and, as in this example, wooden panelling were popular in the second half of the 19th century.*

Stairs

As guests would no longer be expected to go upstairs now the reception rooms were on the ground floor, the stairs in most houses became less prominent and grand compared with Georgian types. The lower section, though, would still have to be impressive. It was just as you reached the first floor that the quality and quantity of moulding and decoration on stairs, doors and walls usually dropped as fittings became plainer, out of sight of visitors. In large Gothic houses the staircase was often sited to one side of the hall, sometimes set within a tower distinguished on the outside by stepped narrow windows and a battlemented or conical roof (see Fig 2.9) or were illuminated by a large stained-glass window or a skylight.

Balustrades came in all manner of styles, imitating staircases from a range of periods and there is no one type which is distinctive of Gothic houses. Imitations of Elizabethan and Jacobean types with closed strings (the treads and balusters being fixed to a side panel

called a string), turned balusters (often thinner than the originals), chunky polished handrails, and a prominent newel post at the bottom all made out of oak or mahogany were common. In the finest examples, carved foliage, heraldic

FIG 5.7: *The finest staircases had large stained or patterned glass windows illuminating the space.*

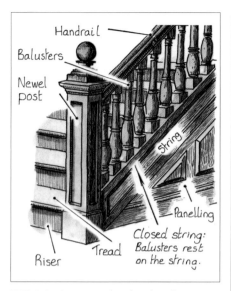

Handrail

Balusters

Newel post

String

Panelling

Closed string: Balusters rest on the string.

Tread

Riser

FIG 5.8: *An example of a closed string staircase in which the balusters rest upon the string rather than an open string version in which they stand directly upon the treads (as seen on left of Fig 5.9).*

symbols, pointed arches and beasts might feature in place of balusters or on top of the newel post. In the largest houses, stone stairs with polished marble columns and foliage capitals or cast-iron balustrades with Gothic symbols and patterns could be found. The treads were usually covered by a runner (a long, thin carpet piece) held in place by brass or iron rods with the exposed sides painted brown or grained if not made from hardwood.

Dining room

The dining room was regarded as a male domain and tended to have strong-coloured decoration and furniture which could be massive but simple in style. A mahogany dining table would be the centre piece, with chairs now usually left beneath it rather than pushed back around the wall as had been the fashion up until the mid 19th century (if this was the case, then a dado to protect the wall

FIG 5.9: *Victorian balustrades used 17th- and 18th-century types for inspiration but happily mixed up parts from different periods. They were generally thinner than the originals.*

FIG 5.10: *A Victorian Gothic-style dining room from a large house, with strong coloured walls to act as a background for paintings, a beamed ceiling, wood panelling over the lower half of the wall and an elaborate sideboard on which the owners could display their finest crockery.*

from chair backs would have been fitted). A sideboard with shelving and cupboards above on which the fine dinnerware could be displayed was desirable, as well as an imposing fireplace in black marble, carved stone or a rich hardwood, with Gothic motifs and foliage decoration. Wooden panelling could be featured in the finest interiors, sometimes just on the lower half with a warm colour like red to offset the paintings hung on the walls or a simple patterned paper in a strong colour above it. A richly-patterned Turkish carpet was highly prized for the dining room although, as with other features in the room, they were readily imitated in cheaper materials for ordinary middle-class homes.

Drawing room

The drawing room (shortened from the earlier 'withdrawing' room) was a lighter more feminine space, where the ladies withdrew to after dinner, while the gentlemen were left behind for often rowdy, drunken discussion. Early Gothic-style ones might have panelling

FIG 5.11: *A mid Victorian drawing room from a middle-class terrace packed with furniture, fittings and ornaments.*

fully or partly covering the walls, while the finest examples had tapestries hung rather than paintings, with embroidered wall hangings replacing these later in the century. Later examples were more likely to be wallpapered, especially in the middle-class home, and from the 1850s this was often done over the complete wall with no dado rail breaking it up but with a larger skirting board and cornice above and beneath. Brass or iron rods for paintings and wall hangings were often used, as picture rails did not become common until the last decades of the century. Although patterns and

colours would still seem busy and dark to modern eyes, they were usually lighter than those used in the dining room, with cream, greens, grey, blues, and lavender being popular.

The furniture in a larger drawing room tended to be arranged in conversational groups, with upholstered chairs and small tables for games or refreshments, a writing desk and display cabinets around the walls, and a piano in a corner. In the more modest middle-class terrace the owner often tried to put much the same content into a smaller space and hence this became the room crammed with the busy patterns, overbearing furniture and large plants with which we associate Victorian interiors. This was made worse as, without a separate library, all manner of books and ornaments would have to be displayed here too. In all examples, the fireplace was the centrepiece of the room, usually in a lighter stone, hardwood or cheaper material imitating the former with a Tudor shallow-arched opening and decorated with Gothic motifs and often a screen to protect those close to it from excessive heat.

Morning/breakfast room

In addition to the two principal reception rooms, most large houses or terraces would have had a separate room for everyday use by the family, titled either a morning or breakfast room. They would be more modest in size and decoration than the drawing and dining room, perhaps with a table and chairs for taking light meals and also with a writing table or a sideboard.

Library

This was an important room where there was space for one to be fitted; a masculine sanctuary where the owner of the house could not only work and study but also impress guests with his fine collection of books, manuscripts and paintings. It was ideally covered in oak panelling, with any exposed wall in a strong coloured paint or paper and glass-door bookcases often featuring pointed arches somewhere in the design. It might also be furnished with a fireplace, a desk, leather-buttoned chairs

and a lectern upon which to display an open book.

Bedrooms

Bedrooms were more than just somewhere to sleep and dress, they were where babies were born, the old or infirm spent much of their day and where the occupants had to wash and relieve themselves as bathrooms and flushing toilets did not become common until the late 19th century. These upstairs rooms now out of sight of most guests were more simply decorated, with less elaborate moulding and plain walls which were painted or papered. They also had movable floor coverings which, as Victorians became more aware of hygiene, made cleaning easier. In the

FIG 5.12: *A mid Victorian bedroom, with lighter, plainer fittings than downstairs. Metal framed beds became popular from the 1860s while washstands, as in the example in the corner, were a must as bathrooms were rare at this date.*

larger house the husband and wife might have separate bedrooms with their own dressing rooms off these, while the four-poster bed with its heavy curtains was replaced at first by half testers with fabric just draped over a canopy at the head of the bed and, from the 1860s, with iron or brass bedsteads.

The main bedrooms were likely to have a small fireplace although this was usually only lit when someone was unwell and for most of the time was left open to aid ventilation. These fireplaces were often made from cast iron, perhaps with Gothic motifs in a simple design. Furniture would include freestanding wardrobes, sometimes with a mirror on the centre door (built-in types were not usually fitted at this date), dressing tables (often covered with lace and trinkets), a washstand with a hand basin

and a chest or couch. Walls tended to be lighter than downstairs, with pinks, greys and greens popular and, later, light floral wallpapers, while the floorboards were polished or painted and covered with carpet pieces, rugs, matting or, by the 1870s, with sheets of linoleum.

Kitchen

The Gothic style would rarely have made an impression in the service rooms. In a larger house there would have been a suite of rooms based around the kitchen for the preparation of food, cooking and cleaning up afterwards, as well as for laundry and in some cases for specialist food production. In most middle-class urban homes from the 1870s, the kitchen was no longer sited in the dark and damp basement but was now in an extension at the rear next to the new mains water and

FIG 5.13: *A mid Victorian kitchen from a large house centred around the cast-iron range (left) and a large table for preparation of food in the middle. Kitchens in this period could have a variety of gadgets, like the warming trolley and portable roaster in front of the range, and the knife polisher on the back wall. Walls would be plain white or cream, and dressers could be hardwood or painted cream, brown or green.*

drainage supplies, usually with a scullery attached where the washing and cleaning took place. As most families of this class would have a cook, the owner rarely spent any time here and hence decoration and style would be simple, with whitewashed and tiled walls, a central preparation table and a cast-iron range.

For those restoring or recreating a Gothic-style house, the kitchen is the one room which has dramatically changed over the past century and a half. Today it is usually the social hub of the house, in effect one of the main reception rooms, with the roles formerly carried out in a series of rooms now combined in this one space thanks to modern appliances. It is also likely to have been extended or moved from its original position. As a result there are few models to base any scheme upon so you have something of a free rein. There are specialist manufacturers who will create pointed-arch kitchen unit doors and Gothic furniture. However, simple framed oak doors with perhaps a castellated cornice and pelmet would be less overpowering, used with suitable paint colours and stencils on the walls to add the style. It would also be appropriate to limit the built-in look to just the main sink and cooker run. A freestanding dresser, larder cupboard and table, perhaps with a utensil rack hanging from above, are features which could be found in original kitchens.

Bathroom

Bathrooms were rare until the 1880s when water pressure was increased so it could be piped upstairs. In most earlier houses, an old back bedroom was converted into a bathroom at a later date. Examples from this period had the bath and other sanitary ware encased in a fine wood boxing. It was only in the

FIG 5.14: *Bathrooms which were fitted in this period tended to have their new fittings boxed in hardwood panelling. It was only in the last few decades of the 19th century that the bath and basin were left open to improve hygiene. This room was popular with the middle classes but less so with the gentry who were often happy to continue having the servants bring hot water to their bath in the bedroom than fit 'new fangled' plumbing.*

FIG 5.15: *An example of a wash basin boxed in original hardwood.*

late 19th century, with growing concern for hygiene, that they were left exposed beneath. Chrome taps and fittings, plain coloured tiles halfway up the wall capped by a thick moulded piece, and a linoleum floor were common at this date. The water closet was always in a separate room, sited downstairs in early examples and only moving up next to the bathroom when water pressure improved. Most people still used earth

closets and chamber pots in this period.

The modern bathroom has these two rooms combined and the addition of showers, storage and, in many, extra room for dressing which was formerly done in the bedroom. As there were few ever built in the Gothic style, anyone recreating one has to use a certain amount of imagination in their scheme, although there are a number of appropriate Victorian glazed, plain coloured tiles, mouldings, wallpapers and stencils available. You could keep it clean and hygienic with the style subtly introduced into the glazed sanitary ware or tiling and a strong patterned flooring, or you could go for strong coloured green or blue wall tiles with stencilled patterns in the walls above and Gothic-style curtains on black iron rods.

FITTINGS AND DECORATION

Walls

Walls in this mid Victorian period grew in height and were often divided by a dado rail three or four feet from the floor, even though it may no longer have been

FIG 5.16: *Leading designers recommended simple two-dimensional designs (left and centre) but despite this, mass-produced patterns which appeared raised from the surface or ones which tried to imitate another material remained popular throughout this period.*

FIG 5.17: *Examples of wall coverings with wallpapers (left), ceramic tiles (top right) and wood panelling (bottom right). Browns, reds and greens were popular but, as in the bottom left example, they did not have to be intense. Note that all the woodwork was painted or grained a dark brown.*

used to protect the plastered surface from chair backs. Some, however, were left undivided by mouldings, with the skirting rising in height and the cornice or coving extending in size, appropriately leaving a large body of wall which would take a strongly-coloured and large patterned paper. The mass production of wallpaper had taken time to develop but by the 1850s continuous rolls with multi-coloured patterns were available for middle-class homes. Early examples were often imitating another surface or were painted to appear that they were raised off the wall, with floral patterns and scenes from famous events or battles seemingly popular, despite the work of Pugin, Owen Jones and other designers in advocating more simple, two dimensional designs. With improved lighting and new chemical dyes darker blues, greens and reds with touches of gold became fashionable, with later papers recreating medieval designs, diaper patterns, simple Gothic motifs or Islamic art. Embossed papers became popular in hardwearing areas from the 1870s.

The most desirable wall covering, however, was wood panelling, full height if you could afford it, half height in the more modest home. It was usually found in the hall, dining room and library and could range from simple plain squares to linenfold (a rippling fabric design) with foliage and heraldic carved details. Oak or mahogany were preferable and used in the finest examples. If cheaper softwoods were used, then painting them was recommended although as with other wooden surfaces many were probably grained to look like a finer timber.

Flooring

In the finest rooms, polished stone or marble, hardwood or parquet floors with imported rugs were desirable, while cheaper softwoods with parquet around the edge and a large carpet piece in the centre was popular in middle-class

homes. Another solution was to paint the floorboards and decorate the exposed parts with stencilling and have oil cloths (large canvas sheets impregnated with size and paint to simulate rugs) or druggets (coarse woven rugs with simple designs) across it. Although fitted carpets had become fashionable for a short period in the 19th century, leaving a gap of a couple of feet around the room was recommended by Gothic designers as it revealed the construction of the floor and meant the covering in the centre could be removed for cleaning.

These carpets were usually patterned, with architects preferring to use simple repeating patterns like diaper diamond designs often in a contrasting colour from the walls although mass-produced versions often had more intense designs, with some imitating Gothic features much to the derision of Pugin. Turkish,

FIG 5.18: *A section of a mid Victorian tiled floor with its distinctive diaper design, punctuated by motifs formed with geometric pieces and a central encaustic tile. Plain red hardwearing tiles called quarries were used around the edge of this design and could be found covering busy service areas of the house.*

Persian or Indian rugs which from the 1870s became widely available were also recommended as they had irregular and colourful designs and an honesty in their production.

The most characteristic flooring in this period and one which can often still be found under layers of later coverings is encaustic and geometric ceramic tiles. Pugin and Henry Minton worked together to revive the medieval art of pouring liquid clay into patterns recessed in the tile and creating encaustic tiles in the 1840s and they began being used in the finest houses. A cheaper method found in middle-class homes was to use geometric-shaped coloured tiles to form busy patterns, perhaps with an occasional encaustic tile inserted in the better examples.

Ceilings

Ceilings in Gothic reception rooms tended to be patterned with either timber beams recreating a 16th-century great chamber or with raised plaster decoration. In some of the finest houses, exotic themes were used to inspire richly-painted creations (see Fig 5.2). In most middle-class houses, cheaper moulded plaster pieces, including ribs, pendants and heraldic designs were arranged and painted, while in less important rooms a cornice and ceiling rose (designed to cover up the marks produced by the lighting hung below) were used.

Internal doors

Although the front door was often formed from vertical planks on a Gothic house, the internal ones would usually be panelled; polished hardwoods in the finest homes and softwood painted in a plain colour or grained in most middle-class homes. Downstairs door furniture could be in brass, black ironwork or a tinned metal finish and was often highly decorative with Gothic-style patterns and motifs. Upstairs, out of sight of guests, the moulding around the door panels might be absent and knobs and finger plates simple mass-produced pieces.

Fireplaces

The fireplace was the centrepiece of any reception room and even in a modest

FIG 5.19: *Early Gothic Revival fireplace surrounds imitated Tudor designs as in this example, with a shallow pointed arch and simple Gothic motifs. Although in some of the finest houses wood was burnt, most had cast-iron register grates inserted for convenience.*

FIG 5.20: *Fireplaces were often draped in fabric which acted as a smoke deflector. After the design of grates and the draw improved making these drapes less necessary, they were often still retained for decorative purposes. The example on the right illustrates the wide range of materials used for fireplace surrounds, in this case with a hardwood, white/grey and black marbles.*

middle-class home would be imposing and decorative. Gothic-style surrounds with a deep shelf above (earlier Georgian ones had shallow tops as they didn't use the space for an array of ornaments) could be made from hardwood, stone or marbles (different coloured ones used together) or from cheaper materials painted to appear like them (slate painted to appear like a polished dark marble). Some were of a conventional form with Gothic motifs, capitals and heraldic symbols plastered upon them; others could be plainer stone types with a shallow pointed arch. In less important rooms, cast-iron one piece or softwood compact surrounds could be found.

Although many Gothic architects designed large open surrounds with brick tiles around a wood burning fire, more convenient, controllable and compact coal grates were usually fitted in middle-

FIG 5.21: *A semi-circular cast-iron register grate which was a distinctive design popular in the 1850s and '60s.*

FIG 5.22: *In bedrooms, smaller cast-iron grates with a compact basket for the coals were often fitted as in this example. However, they were rarely lit and usually only used when someone old or infirm was occupying the room. Smaller bedrooms may have had no fireplace at all, while others may have been removed at a later date when central heating was installed. (Calculating the number of flues or chimney pots can often help to work out which rooms were originally heated or not.)*

large semi-circular arched types with rounded sides intended to reflect more of the heat from the fire back into the room became fashionable in the 1850s and '60s. From the 1870s, rectangular castings with tiled side cheeks and a short canopy above the basket which was set further forward to give off more heat became popular.

Furniture

Gothic-style furniture could range from the elaborate overworked pieces covered in all manner of medieval motifs to more simple pieces recommended by designers like Pugin, which were inspired by sturdy Jacobean work. Sideboards, bookcases and display cabinets tended to be richly decorated and even in the hands of leading designers could become a riot of carving, with pointed arches formed in the doors and foliage, quatrefoils and mouldings around the

FIG 5.23: *A Gothic-style chair incorporating pointed arches in the design.*

class homes. The grate set within the surround was changing during this period as ones with an adjustable flap covering the opening to the chimney to control the draw, the register, became a standard fitting. Improvements were also made to the design of the grate, with

FIG 5.24: *A distinctive upholstered chair from this period, with a simple Gothic-designed fabric.*

sides and on supports. Oak was the most desirable material and could be constructed in such a way as to show the nature of its structure and how the joints were formed. It was used to make traditional furniture like refectory tables, settles and chairs. In more modest homes, copies of 17th-century pieces in other woods like mahogany were used. Rectangular tables often had distinctive rounded corners and bulbous legs while chairs and settees could have a buttoned covering from the 1850s. With upholstery, the focus was upon the material, with velvets trimmed with plain silk or specially produced medieval-style fabrics used on simple designed pieces rather than the flamboyant rich sofas which were popular at the time. From the mid 19th century, bedroom suites began to be introduced in mahogany, walnut and rosewoods, some with a simple Gothic design, with lighter woods used from the

FIG 5.25: *A Victorian dining table, with distinctive curved corners and bulbous legs.*

1870s. In the 1860s, cottage-style furniture devoid of fussy decoration began to be introduced, while in the following decade Aesthetic-style pieces inspired by Japanese types began to influence furniture design.

Curtains

In most homes curtains were a series of layers, each designed not only for privacy but also to reduce draughts and protect furnishings from sunlight. It was also common for heavyweight types used in winter months to be replaced by lighter versions in summer. Gothic designers advocated a much more simple approach and were happy for there to be just one set of curtains hung from a metal or wooden rail, with a valance to trim the top. The fabrics used included velvets, damasks and simple prints, with heraldic motif designs and a plain fringe.

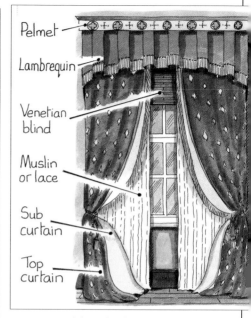

FIG 5.27: *Although advocating simple window treatments, it is likely that in many Gothic Revival houses, the traditional multi-layered arrangement as pictured here was still used during this period. This was for practical reasons as the blinds, lace and sub curtains helped to protect delicate fabrics and furniture in the room from fading in direct sunlight and also provided privacy during the day.*

FIG 5.26: *A Gothic-style fabric with simple repeating pattern, as advocated by leading designers. As with wallpaper, busy florals and three-dimensional effects were widely used in this period.*

They were hung (without any fancy festoons) down to and flowing slightly over the floor and held at the sides with metal tie backs.

Lighting

Victorian homes were lit by a combination of light sources. Gas lights had only become popular since their use

FIG 5.28: *Examples of a gas ceiling light and oil lamp from this period.*

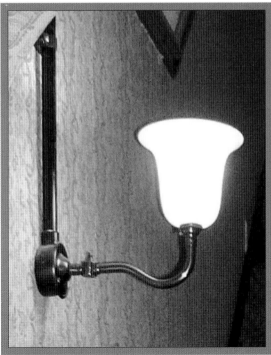

FIG 5.29: *Wall-mounted gas lights became popular in houses from the 1850s. Earlier types had the light facing up, while later in the century improved mantles which were brighter and could point down were developed.*

in the Houses of Parliament and there would only be a limited number of fittings at this date, with the mantle pointing upwards (downward facing mantles were introduced in the 1880s). Oil lamps were common, with improved versions using paraffin introduced in the 1840s, while candles were still widely used by all classes, with beeswax types reserved for special occasions. Inspiration for the design of some light fittings, oil lamps, chandeliers and candlesticks came from medieval halls, with large wooden rings of candles hung on chains or from the polished metalwork pieces found in churches. Victorian versions used brass, bronze, and wrought iron, with decorative chandeliers in the main reception rooms, a lantern or wall sconces in the hall and simple lamps or candles upstairs. Although gas and oil lighting was brighter than the types used in earlier periods, it was still only a fraction of the brightness of a modern electric bulb. Yet, coupled with the strong coloured walls, enhanced the rich tones and simple luxury of a fine Gothic interior.

FIG 5.30: *Floors, with plain, geometric shapes and encaustic patterned tiles are a distinctive feature of Gothic houses, as in this example from a modest terrace with distinctive browns, beiges, reds and blues.*

PLACES TO VISIT

Despite our love of old buildings and the popularity of the style, there are surprisingly few Gothic Revival houses open to the public. Most of those shown in this book are private homes or have been converted into hotels, schools or for other uses. There are, however, a number of country properties and suburban homes listed below dating from this period which contain elements of the style that can help capture the atmosphere of mid and late Victorian interiors.

Brantwood, Coniston, Cumbria LA21 8AD, tel. 015394 41396, www.brantwood.org.uk
John Ruskin's house which he bought in 1871. Although not of this period, it contains some alterations by him and interiors recreated as they may have been in his day.

Cardiff Castle, Castle Street, Cardiff CF10 3RB, tel. 029 2087 8100, www.cardiffcastle.com (Fig 2.8).
A Norman castle which William Burges extended to create a huge Gothic mansion with outstanding interiors.

Carlyle's House, 24 Cheyne Row, Chelsea, London SW3 5HL, tel. 020 7352 7087, (National Trust) www.nationaltrust.org.uk
The home from 1834–1867 of Thomas and Jane Carlyle, with notable period interiors.

Castell Coch, Castle Road, Tongwynlais, Cardiff CF15 7JS, tel. 029 2081 0101, cadw.wales.gov.uk (Fig 5.1).
Burges's fairytale medieval-style castle, with interiors to match those of nearby Cardiff Castle.

Cragside, Rothbury, Northumberland NE65 7PX, tel. 01699 620333, (National Trust) www.nationaltrust.org. (Fig 2.18).
Norman Shaw's Old English-style mansion.

Emery Walker's House, 7 Hammersmith Terrace, London W6 9TS, tel. 0208 741 4104, www.emerywalker.org.uk.
Well-preserved Arts and Crafts interiors.

The Grange, St Augustine's Road, Ramsgate, Kent CT11 9NY, tel. 01628 825925, www.landmarktrust.org.uk. (Fig 2.14).
Pugin's house is available as holiday accommodation but is also open for visiting a few days in the year. Check the website for dates.

Knightshayes Court, Bolham, Tiverton EX16 7RQ, tel. 01884 257381, (National Trust) www.nationaltrust.org.uk .
A modest-sized Gothic country house by William Burges, although disagreement with the owner meant his interiors were never fully executed.

Holker Hall and Gardens, Cark-in-Cartmel, Grange-over-Sands, Cumbria LA11 7PL, tel. 01539 558328, www.holker.co.uk.
Elizabethan Gothic-style house largely rebuilt after a fire in 1871, with some excellent period interiors.

Hughenden Manor, High Wycombe, Bucks, HP14 4LA, tel. 01494 755573 (National Trust) www.nationaltrust.org.uk
Disraeli's house, remodelled by E.B. Lamb in his unique style, with Gothic elements and interiors as they may have appeared in the 1860s.

There are also a number of museums and galleries which have collections of art, furnishings and furniture from this period:

Birmingham Museum and Art Gallery, Chamberlain Square, Birmingham B3 3DH, tel. 0121 303 2834, www.bmag.org.uk

Brighton Museum & Art Gallery, Royal Pavilion Gardens, Brighton BN1 1EE, tel. 03000 290900, www.brighton-hove-rpml.org.uk

The Museum of Domestic Design and Architecture, Middlesex University, Cat Hill, Barnet, Hertfordshire, EN4 8HT, tel. 0208 411 5244. www.moda.mdx.ac.uk

Victoria and Albert Museum, Cromwell Road, London SW7 2RL, tel. 0207 942 2000, www.vam.ac.uk

The Whitworth Art Gallery, Oxford Road, Manchester M15 6ER, tel. 0161 275 7450, www.whitworth.man.ac.uk

USEFUL WEBSITES

Unfortunately, many houses from this period have had their original doors and windows removed, often in recent decades, in the erroneous belief that they cannot be upgraded to modern standards. This not only spoils the appearance and lowers the long-term value of the property but also replacement with good quality uPVC parts is usually more expensive than upgrading the existing fittings. There are local builders and national companies (who can be accessed via the internet) who can restore and upgrade sash windows and original doors to improve heat retention, noise reduction and security without the loss of fittings which have survived in some cases for over 150 years and will last far longer than modern plastic versions which are often replaced after only 20 years. There is also a wide range of reclamation yards and auction houses where original fittings and furnishings can be purchased; most with websites that can be found via your search engine. There is also now a growing number of manufacturers who produce original fittings like windows and doors for period homes which are authentic in appearance and meet modern security and emissions standards. Below are listed some of the websites which can help you find out more about Victorian houses and suitable fittings and decoration when renovating.

www.bricksandbrass.co.uk
www.victorianweb.org.uk
www.littlegreene.com
www.terracedhouses.co.uk
www.victoriansociety.org.uk
www.periodproperty.co.uk
www.channel4.com/4homes
www.bbc.co.uk/homes/design
www.salvo.co.uk
www.lpoc.co.uk (The Listed Property Owners Club)
www.english-heritage.org.uk

GLOSSARY

architrave	The moulding around a door, window or niche.
ashlar	Large blocks of stone cut square with fine joints.
baluster	Plain or decorated post supporting the stair rail. A balustrade is a row of balusters with a rail along the top.
bargeboard	External vertical boards which protect the ends of the sloping roof on a gable and often decorated.
bay window	A window projecting from the façade of a house of varying height but always resting on the ground.
bitumen	A petroleum derivative used for waterproofing flat roofs and forming a damp proof layer in walls or under floors.
bond	The way bricks are laid in a wall, with the different patterns formed by alternative arrangements of headers (the short ends) and stretchers (the long side).
bow window	A bay window with a curved profile.
buttress	A vertical support angled up against a wall. Arts and Crafts types tended to have a steep slope down its full height.
cames	Lead work which holds the small panes (quarries) of glass in a window.
casement window	A window which is hinged along one side.
cast iron	A brittle metal formed in moulds, whereas wrought iron is pliable and forged into decorative patterns.
cornice	A decorative moulding which runs around the top of an external or internal wall.
dado	The lower section of a wall. The moulding along the top of this is the dado rail.
damp proof membrane (DPM)	A waterproof barrier incorporated within walls and ground floors to stop rising damp penetrating the structure above.
dormer window	A window projecting out of the roof with a flat or gabled top.
eaves	The section of the roof timbers under the tiles or slates where they meet the wall, usually protected by a fascia board.
façade	The main vertical face of the house.
flue	The duct for smoke from the fireplace up into the chimney.

frieze	The horizontal strip of decoration above the picture rail. In this period it was often a paper complementing the wallpaper below. In Arts and Crafts houses it was often painted white.
gable	The pointed upper section of wall at the end of a pitched roof. A Dutch gable is shaped with concave and convex curves.
Gothic	Medieval architecture which used the pointed arch.
Gothic Revival	The rediscovery of Gothic architecture which was championed by Pugin and Ruskin, and which dominated building from the 1850s to the 1870s.
Gothick	A less accurate and more whimsical form of Gothic which was popular in the late 18th and early 19th century. It was characterised by wide-arched windows with 'Y'-shaped tracery.
hanging tiles	Clay tiles hung vertically off thin strips of wood to cover walls and used by Arts and Crafts architects for its visual appeal.
herringbone	Brickwork laid in a zig-zag.
hipped roof	A roof with a slope on all four sides.
inglenook	A recessed space for a fire, with seating to the sides.
jambs	The sides of an opening for a door or window.
jetty	The projection of an upper storey of a timber-framed building.
joggle	Stone blocks with a notch on one face and matching recess on the other to prevent them slipping (see Figs 5.6 and 5.8).
joists	Timber, concrete or steel beams which support the floor.
lintel	A flat beam which is fitted above a door or window to take the load of the wall above.
load bearing	A wall which has to support a load, usually floors and a roof.
mansard roof	A roof formed from two slopes at a different angle, with a profile like the top of a 50p coin, which allows more height for a room within.
moulding	A decorative strip of wood, stone or plaster.
mullion	The vertical member dividing up a window. A low, long window with only mullions is known as a mullion window.
oriel window	A projecting window on an upper storey.
panelling	Wooden lining of interior walls, with vertical muntins and horizontal rails framing the panels.
parapet	The top section of a wall which continues above the sloping end of the roof.

pargetting	Patterns raised or incised in plaster on the exterior surface of a house.
pebbledash	Render with small pebbles and stones thrown against it while drying.
pilaster	A flat column.
pitch	The angle by which a roof slopes. A plain sloping roof of two sides is called a pitched roof.
pointed arch	An arch formed from two curved sections meeting at a point at the top. Early medieval types tend to be upright and narrow, later ones became more shallow and wider.
purlins	Large timbers which run the length of the roof supporting the rafters.
quoins	Raised or highlighted stones up the corner of a building.
rafters	Timbers which are set in a row along the slope of the roof with laths running across their upper surface onto which the tiles are fixed.
render	A protective covering for a wall made from two or three layers of cement.
reveal	The sides (jambs) of a recessed window or door opening.
roughcast	A render with small stones mixed within to give a rough texture when dried.
screed	A mix of sand and cement used to pour over and form the upper layer of the ground floor. Tiles or carpet was fitted directly to its dried surface.
string	The side support panel for a staircase.
string course	A horizontal band running across a façade and usually projecting.
terracotta	Fine clay moulded and fired into decorative pieces, usually left unglazed on Arts and Crafts buildings.
tracery	The stone ribs forming geometric shapes and intersecting patterns in the upper half of a medieval window.
truss	An arrangement of timber or steel pieces incorporating triangles to form a long beam or support for a roof. When carefully designed, they can stretch further than a single beam.
vernacular	Buildings made from local materials in styles and method of construction passed down within a distinct area, as opposed to architect-designed structures made from mass-produced materials.
weatherboarding	Overlapping horizontal planks used to protect timber-framed structures from the elements and used by Arts and Crafts architects for its visual appeal.

INDEX

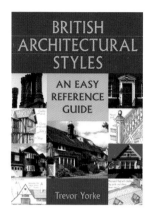

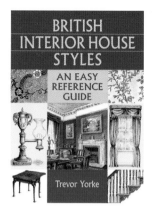

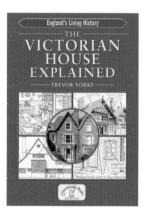

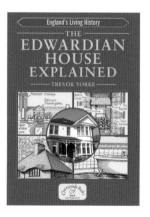

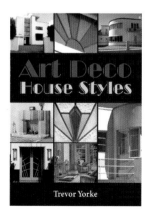

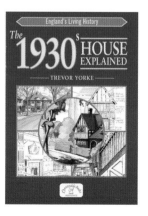

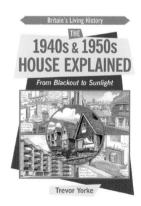